Must-Know Spanish Travel Phrases for a Fun Trip

Learn How to Be Polite, Book a Table at the Restaurant, Ask for Directions, and much more in any Spanish-Speaking Country (English to Spanish)

By: Alina Alonso

Introduction: Basic Facts About Spanish

Spanish is the second most-spoken language in the world and the official language for several countries like Argentina, Bolivia, Chile, Colombia, Cuba, Ecuador, Guatemala, Honduras, Mexico, Panama, Paraguay, Spain, Venezuela, and Uruguay, among many others. But Spanish is also frequently used in some areas of the USA like Los Angeles, Miami, New York, just to name a few.

Therefore, knowing some basic Spanish offers the possibility of interaction with lots of people worldwide!

Before we start learning some phrases to get around in a Spanish-speaking place, there are some things about the language that you should learn. As in any language, Spanish has its easy stuff, but there is some tough stuff. So first, before anything, you should familiarize yourself with some basic facts about the language.

Pronunciation

As Spanish is very different from English, it is important to consider some things about pronunciation. For example, in Spanish, vowels are pronounced clearly and distinctly, like **a** as in **f**ather, **e** as in **e**lephant, **i** as in police, **o** as in **no** and **u** as in **ru**le. In the case of diphthongs, you have to remember to pronounce **ai** as in **ri**se, **ei** as in **day**, **io** as in **yo**ga, **ue** as in **whe**n, **uo** as in **wo**rk and **ui** as in **wee**k. In the case of consonants, some are very similar to English, but some are not. Because of that, you should consider that: **gü** is as in **Gw**en, **ll** as **j**ar, **ñ** as on**i**on, **v** as in **b**oy, **h** is silent, **d** between vowels is pronounced as **th**in, **r** at the beginning of a sentence is pronounced as double r. These pronunciations are the things you should take into account, but the rest of the consonants are exactly like English.

Accents in Spanish are used to mark stress over certain vowels like **pronunciación** or they may be used to differ two identical words that have different meanings, **esta** (that one) from **está** (is). Moreover, as in every other language, there are different pronunciations between countries and persons. Mainly, you will find this differences between people from Spain and people from South America. One important difference is the **c** and **z**, which in

Latin America will be pronounced as **s**oup but in Spain will be pronounced as **th**ought. The other very frequent variation is the **ll** and you can find it pronounced like the **lli** as in million, the **j** in **j**uice, the **sh** in **sh**ow or the **s** in plea**s**ure, depending on where the person you are listening to comes from.

Vocabulary

Although you may find it strange, English is very similar to Spanish in particular aspects. First of all, Spanish comes from Latin, so the words in that language tend to have Latin roots. Similarly, English also has some words which have Latin roots. Therefore, this words will be similar to Spanish. A number of examples are **centro** (center), **museo** (museum), **diferente** (different), **estudiar** (study), among many others. Another resemblance between English and Spanish are

the endings in some words like **profesión**
(profession), **general** (general), **posible**
(possible), **conversación** (conversation), just
to name a few.

But, despite that the other words are
considerably different from English, with
some practice you can become a pro in no
time.

Grammar

However, in grammar, Spanish tends to
differentiate a lot from English as it has some
elements that English does not possess. For
example, nouns in Spanish are either
masculine or feminine, and although there can
be some exceptions, masculine tend to end
with an **-o** and feminine tend to conclude with
an **-a**.

The articles that correspond to the masculine are **el** (he, definite article) or **un** (a, indefinite article), for example, **el gato** (the cat). And the articles that correspond to feminine nouns are **la** (she, definite articles) or **una** (indefinite article), for example, **la casa** (the house). In the case of adjectives, they agree both in gender and number with the nouns and articles, for example, **la casa linda** (the beautiful house) or **el gran equilibrista** (the great equilibrist).

Another thing about Spanish is that there are two forms for the second person both in singular and in plural which vary concerning formality. One is more polite and shows more respect, **usted** (you, singular) and **ustedes** (you, plural), and the other is more informal and shows closeness between speakers, **tu** (singular) and **ustedes** (used in Latin

America)/**vosotros** (used in Spain) (both in plural).

Spanish verbs are highly inflected and tend to have different endings for every person in all the different tenses. Due to this richness in conjugation, the Spanish language can construct sentences without an express subject. This is because the information about who speaks is already contained in the verb, for example, **fueron a comer** (they went to eat) does not provide the express subject that is **ellos** (they) but it is already implied in the ending of **fueron** (went). Also, verbs in Spanish are grouped into three broad categories of conjugation: **-ar**, **-er**, -**ir**. However, many common verbs are irregular.

Another difference with English is that an inverted mark precedes question marks and exclamation marks, in the case of the question

an inverted question mark (**¿Cómo estas?**-
How are you?) and, in the case of
exclamations, by an exclamation mark (**¡hola!**-
Hello!).

Taken this into account, you can start learning
more about Spanish and how to use it. It may
seem hard, but you will see that as the chapters
go by you will get more used to the language
and in no time you will start saying phrases of
all kinds in Spanish. So, **¡Empecemos!** (Let's
start!).

Chapter 1: Basic Phrases

As any traveler arriving at any country whose language is not the same as yours, you should first start learning some basic phrases.

Greetings

First, you should be aware how to greet as it is important for any sort of situation abroad. In Spanish, you can say hello by saying **hola**. Also, you can refer to different times of the day, as in good morning, good afternoon and good evening, by saying in Spanish **buen día**, **buenas tardes** y **buenas noches** (accordingly). And, when you meet someone you may want to tell them **mucho gusto** (it is nice to meet you) or **un placer** (it is a pleasure).

You can also ask someone how they are doing by saying the phrase: **¿Cómo estas?** (how are you?). The possible replies to this question are **bien** (good or fine), **muy bien** (very well), **más o menos** (so-so) and **mal** (bad). In case you are asked and you want to know about how the person is you can reply by describing how you are and then add, **¿y vos?** (and you?).

Moreover, you can ask for someone's name by saying **¿Cómo te llamás?** (what is your name?) or **¿Cuál es tu nombre?** (what is your name?). And you can easily reply to that question by saying **mi nombre es**… (my name is) and your answer. And if you want to say where you are from, you simply say, **yo soy de/nosotros somos de**... (I am from/we come from) and complete with your nationality. For example, **yo soy de Inglaterra** (I am from England) or

nosotros somos de Estados Unidos de America (we are from the USA).

To say goodbye, you can also say it with various phrases such as **adiós** (goodbye), **hasta pronto** (see you soon) y **buenas noches** (good night).

Politeness

Like in any other language and every situation, in order to communicate you need to be polite to the person you are talking to. Some important words to know in Spanish are **si** (yes) and **no** (no). Moreover, you can ask for something by saying **por favor** (please) and thank someone by saying **gracias** (thank you). And if you want to thank someone very emphatically you say **muchas gracias** (thank you very much). In any case, if you feel you are interrupting someone, or you want to apologize, you can start by saying **perdone** o

disculpe (pardon me/excuse me), or you can also say **lo siento** (I am sorry).

If you do not understand when someone is talking to you, you can respond in several ways and use several phrases. First, you can say **no entiendo** (I do not understand) or **yo no hablo español** (I do not speak Spanish). Then, you can ask them if they talk in English by saying **¿Habla ingles?** (do you speak English?). Finally, if you want someone to repeat something you just say **repita, por favor** (repeat, please) or **¿podría repetirme por favor?** (could you repeat that please?). And, if you want someone to talk slower, you can tell them **hable más despacio por favor** (talk slower please) or **¿podría hablar más despacio por favor?** (could you talk slower please?). In any case, you can also ask someone to write down something for you by saying **¿lo**

podría escribir por favor? (can you write it down, please?) or **¿me lo podría escribir por favor?** (could you write it down, please?).

Asking and telling things

If you need any help, you can say **¿me podrías ayudar?** (can you help me?). And, for example, if you want to know where something is you have to start by saying **¿Donde esta…?** (Where is…?) and then you add what you want to know. For example, you can ask someone **¿dónde está el baño?** (where is the bathroom?). Later in this book, you will get more information about directions and how to understand them but for now, on let's continue with some basic things.

Also, you may need to ask certain things, and these are some essential phrases to accomplish that. For example, you can ask **¿ A qué hora**

es…? (What time is…?), or maybe you need to know where some event is taking place by saying **¿Cuándo?** (when?). For example: **¿A qué hora es el concierto?** (what time is the concert?) or **¿cuándo es el concierto?** (when is the concert?). Or if you want any more information you can ask **¿por qué?** (why?) or **¿Podría darme más información, por favor?** (could you give me more details, please?).

However, something crucial to get around in any Spanish speaking country, like any other country, are the verbs **querer** (want), **necesitar** (need) y **tener** (have). With these three verbs, you can easily construct a very significant number of sentences. For example, **yo quiero un taxi** (I want a taxi), **yo necesito un boleto** (I need a ticket), **yo tengo una reservación** (I have a reservation), and so on.

You can also say you like something by saying **me gusta**… (I like…) or **no me gusta…** (I do not like). For example, **me gusta la pizza pero no me gusta el pescado** (I like pizza, but I do not like fish).

Numbers

The numbers in Spanish are **uno** (one), **dos** (two), **tres** (three), **cuatro** (four), **cinco** (five), **seis** (six), **siete** (seven), **ocho** (eight), **nueve** (nine), **diez** (ten), **once** (eleven), **doce** (twelve), **trece** (thirteen), **catorce** (fourteen), **quince** (fifteen), **dieciseis** (sixteen), **diecisiete** (seventeen), **dieciocho** (eighteen), **diecinueve** (nineteen), **veinte** (twenty). Some other numbers you might need are **cincuenta** (fifty), **cien** (a hundred) and **mil** (a thousand). The rest of the numbers you can construct them like sixteen onwards, for example, **veintiseis**, **cincuenta y dos**, etc. Numbers can be hard in Spanish, but you can easily get around with the ones included here.

Other essential information

You can mention the days and the passing of them as **hoy** (today), **mañana** (tomorrow) or **ayer** (yesterday). Moreover, you can refer to **la semana pasada** (last week), **la proxima semana** (next week) or even to el **mes pasado** (last month) or **el proximo mes** (next month).

An essential phrase for when something of any kind goes wrong is **¡no funciona!** (It does not work). It is not sophisticated, but anyone will understand what you want to say, ultimately, that something is not working. Also, in a similar case you may say **hubo un error con**... (there has been some mistake with...) and then you add the thing that went wrong. For example, **hubo un error con mi reserva** (there has been a mistake with my reservation).

In the case of any emergency, you can ask for help by saying either **¡socorro!** (help!), **¡ayuda!** (help!), **¡pare!** (stop!) or **¡vayase!** (go away!). Also, you may ask someone to call the police by saying **llame a la policía** (call the police) or **¿Podría llamar a la policía?** (could you call the police?). This question is similar if you want to ask for an ambulance, for example. In that case, you would say, **llame a una ambulancia** (call an ambulance) or **¿podría llamar a una ambulancia?**. And, finally, if you want to say you are lost you just simply say **estoy perdido** (I am lost).

In this chapter, you have learned the first few basic phrases of Spanish. These will serve you in any situation and are elemental to communicate in any sort of a Spanish speaking environment. You can now greet someone and ask them how you are doing, you can say your name and ask for others, you can be polite by saying please and thank you. Moreover, you can communicate in case something is not right, you can also build some basic phrases with simple verbs, you know how to count, and more.

Keywords: **Hola** (hello), **¿cómo estás?** (how are you?), **si** (yes), **no** (no), **porfavor** (please), **gracias** (thank you), **disculpas** (I am sorry), **¿me podrías ayudar?** (can you help me?), **ayuda** (help), **estoy perdido** (I am lost).

Chapter 2: Getting There And Being There

Now that you have some basic phrases, you need to know how to get around to the first situations you are going to encounter in a Spanish-speaking country or environment. For that purpose, this chapter will help you with anything you might need to resolve at the airport or when you first arrive at your hotel.

Airport

When you get to the airport, the first thing you need to do is to check-in. There, you can ask for your seat preferences by saying **prefiero un asiento de pasillo** (I prefer an aisle seat) or **prefiero un asiento de ventana** (I prefer a window seat). And, you can say how much luggage you are travelling with **tengo … maletas** (I have … suitcases). In that situation, you can complete with the number you are carrying, for example, **tengo dos maletas** (I have two suitcases). You can also refer to your carry-on luggage by saying **equipaje de mano**. Therefore you can say **ese es mi equipaje de mano** (that is my carry-on luggage) or **¿puedo llevar esto como equipaje de mano?** (can I take this as carry-on luggage?).

Once you pass this stage and airport security, you should find your terminal and get ready for your flight. In case you cannot find it you can say, **busco la terminal…** (and you insert your number) (I am looking for terminal number…). For example, **busco la terminal nueve** (I am looking for terminal number nine). You can also ask if it is the international terminal by saying **¿esta terminal es para vuelos internacionales?** (Is this terminal for international flights?).

And, when you get to your terminal and your gate you might have some other questions regarding the flight. For example, if there is any problem you can ask **¿Por qué tarda tanto?** (why is it taking so long?) or you may ask directly to a staff member **¿Cuánto tiempo habrá de retraso?** (how long will it be delayed?). You can also ask other things about the flight like **¿es un vuelo directo?** (Is it a direct flight?) or **¿ Cuánto dura el vuelo a …?** (How long is the flight to…?). Finally, if you have a problem with your boarding pass you may say, **hay un problema con mi pase de abordar** (there is a problem with my boarding pass) or **perdí mi pase de abordar** (I lost my boarding pass).

Then, you will get to your destination and here is where your Spanish practice really begins. For example, if you need some help with your things, you can use luggage carts, but if you cannot find them you can ask **¿Dónde están los carritos de equipaje?** (Where are the luggage carts?). In case you cannot find where to pick your luggage you can ask someone by saying, **¿en qué banda puedo recoger mi equipaje?** (from which conveyor belt can I pick my luggage?). But if you have any problems you should not hesitate and contact some airport staff. You can tell them **mis maletas no llegaron** (my luggage has not arrived), **mis maletas se perdieron** (my luggage is lost), or **no se donde estan mis maletas** (I do not know where my luggage is).

Finally, you are almost ready to leave the airport. But first, you need to pass some controls. You may need to use some phrases like, **¿Dónde está la aduana?** (Where is customs?) or **No tengo nada que declarar** (I have nothing to declare). If you are asked any questions, you can reply to them by saying if you are travelling alone or with someone by saying **estoy viajando solo** (I am travelling alone), or **estoy viajando con** … (I am travelling with…). For example, you can say **estoy viajando con mi esposa** (I am travelling with my wife). You can also state the purpose of your trip by saying **estoy aqui…** (I am here) and then you can complete it with your own information. For example, **estoy aqui de vacaciones** (I am here on holiday) or **estoy aqui de negocios** (I am here on business). Furthermore, you can say how long you are staying with the phrase **voy a estar…** (I am here for…). And then you can complete it with your own information, for example, **voy a estar**

dos semanas (I am here for two weeks) or **voy a estar por cinco días** (I am here for five days).

Hotel and accommodations

Now that you made it to your hotel or desired accommodation, you might need to know some basic phrases for you to get settled. For example, if you did not make a reservation you can go to the lobby and say **Quisiera reservar una habitación, por favor** (I would like to book a room, please). You can ask for **una habitación sencilla** (a single room) or **una habitación doble** (a double room). Also, you can ask for the cost by saying **¿Cuánto cuesta?** (How much is it?) and if you have more particular requests you can say, for example, **¿Cuánto cuesta una habitación doble por tres noches?** (How much is a double room for two nights?). Moreover, if you want separate beds you should say, **¿Cuánto cuestan las**

camas individuales? (How much are the separate beds?) or **¿Tenes una habitación con camas individuales?** (do you have a room with separate beds?). If you want to know more about the accommodations of the rooms you can ask **¿Tiene una habitación con baño?** (do you have a room with bathroom?) or **¿Tiene una habitación con aire acondicionado?** (do you have a room with air conditioner?).

If you want, you can ask to see the room by saying, **¿Podría ver la habitación?** (can I see the room?). And, if you if you want to take it and stay there, you say **esta bien, la tomo** (It is fine, I will take it) and if you want to see another room you can ask **¿podría ver otra habitación?** (can I see another room?).

As you are making your reservation, you might encounter with some doubts about the payment and the hotel hours and facilities. For example, if you want to know if they accept credit cards you can ask **¿aceptan tarjetas de credito?** (do you take credit cards?). Also, if you want to know about the payment you can ask **¿Necesito pagar por adelantado?** (do I have to pay upfront?) or **¿puedo pagar después?** (can I pay later?). To ask about some facilities you can say, **¿Cuándo se sirve el desayuno?** (when is the breakfast served?), **¿Hay una lavandería aquí?** (Is there a laundry room here?), **¿Puedo usar la piscina?** (May I use the swimming pool?). And if you want the person at the reception to wake you at any given hour you may tell them, **porfavor, despierteme a las**… (please wake me at…) and you tell them your desired time, for example, **por favor, despierteme a las ocho de la mañana** (please, wake me at eight in the morning).

If you have any problems at the hotel, you can quickly solve them with these phrases. For example, you can say **Disculpas** (I am sorry) or **Tengo un problema** (I have a problem), and then you tell them your situation, like **perdí mi llave** (I lost my key) or **el ventilador no funciona** (the fan does not work). Some other problems may be, **no hay toallas en mi habitación** (there are no towels in my room), **las toallas no estan limpias** (the towels are not clean) or **¿Podría darme otra manta?** (could you give me another blanket?). Further complaints might be: **hay mucho ruido** (it is very noisy), **la habitación es muy oscura** (the room is very dark), **la televisión no funciona** (the tv does not work), **no hay agua caliente en el baño** (there is no hot water in the bathroom), **esta habitación huele muy mal** (this room smells very bad), and **¿podría**

cambiar de habitación? (Can I change rooms?).

Finally, regarding your accommodation vocabulary, you may need to know some phrases for when you leave the place. If you want to know when is the check-out you can say, **¿hasta qué hora es el check-out?** (until what time is the check-out?). Furthermore, if you need some more time in the hotel, you can ask by saying, **¿podría dejar la habitación más tarde?** (can I check out later?) or if you want to leave your bags some time you can ask **¿Puedo dejar mi equipaje hasta las…?** (Can I leave my luggage until…?). Also, you can ask, **¿ podría llamarme un taxi al aeropuerto?** (could you call me a taxi to the airport?). And you thank them by saying, **¡Muchas gracias! Tuve una estancia muy agradable** (Thanks! I had a pleasant stay).

In this chapter, you have learned some really useful phrases for when you travel, and these refer to flight and hotel situations. These phrases show how to get around and how to communicate in those environments and in case anything happens that you need to resolve. Among many things, you have learned the vocabulary to check in on a flight and ask how to get to your terminal, how to ask if there are any problems with the check, how to handle costumes. Moreover, you know how to arrange a reservation at an accommodation place, how to complain in case your accommodation has any problems and how to thank for your stay.

Keywords: **asiento** (seat), **terminal** (terminal), **maleta** (luggage), **equipaje de mano** (carry-on luggage), **habitación** (room), **noches** (nights), **¿podría llamarme un taxi?** (can you call me a taxi?).

Chapter 3: Sightseeing

Now that you are settled in, you are ready to explore and look around your Spanish speaking destination! You should know how to get from place to place and ask for directions and addresses if needed.

Directions

In order to move around your Spanish speaking site you may need to ask for directions, know basic vocabulary about transportation and, most importantly, learn how to understand these instructions and transportation. You already know how to ask **¿Dónde?** (where?) and with this, you can ask for many things like **¿Dónde estan los taxis?** (where are the taxis?), **¿Por dónde pasa el autobús?** (Where is the bus?), **¿Dónde está el metro?** (Where is the subway?) and **¿Dónde está la salida?** (where is the exit?), among many others.

You may also ask **¿Esta cerca?** (Is it near?), **¿Esta lejos?** (Is it far) or **¿ A qué distancia está?** (how far is it?) referring to a place or street. You can ask to be taken somewhere by saying **lleveme a esta dirección, por favor** (take me to this address, please) or you may ask if some bus goes to a particular place by saying **¿Pasa este autobus por la calle…?** (does this bus go to … street?). In a taxi, you can also ask **¿Cuánto está la tarifa?** (how much is the fare?) and you can tell the driver to stop by saying **detengase aquí, por favor** (stop here, please).

If you want to ask for a map you can do it by saying **un plano de la ciudad, por favor** (a city map, please) or **un plano del metro, por favor** (a map of the subway, please). Also, you can ask for a particular street by saying, **busco esta calle** (I am looking for this street). Or, you can even ask for the location of certain spots like: **¿Hay un supermercado por aquí?** (Is there a supermarket around here?), **¿Hay un banco por aquí?** (Is there a bank around here?), **¿Cómo llego a la catedral?** (how do I get to the cathedral?), **¿Puedo caminar al centro desde aquí?** (can I walk to the center from here?).

Now that you know how to ask for basic instructions it is crucial that you know how to understand them clearly, as they are your tools for getting around this unfamiliar place. If someone tells you to **siga derecho** it means to go straight ahead and if they say **vaya en esa dirección** it means to go that way. You might be told **vuelva** (go back), **vaya a la derecha** (go right) o **vaya a la izquierda** (go left). Also if you ask for a train station they may answer you by saying **la estación de tren está en esa dirección** (the train station is that way) or if you ask which station to get off the train they may answer, for example, **baje en la… estación** (get off at… station).

If someone tells you **está demasiado lejos para caminar**, it means that It is too far for you to walk there. They may also say **vaya por acá** (go this way) o **siga derecho hasta la intersección** (go straight until the intersection).

Sightseeing

When you first start looking around you might need some phrases in order to know more about the place you are visiting. For example, you can ask almost everything by saying **¿Qué es eso?** (what is that?) o **¿Qué es ese edificio?** (what is that building?). If you are touring around or looking at touristic places like museums and landmarks you might find some doubts regarding the places. To respond them you can quickly ask, for example, **¿ A qué hora abren?** (what time does it open?) or **¿A qué hora cierran?** (what time do you close?). Some other important questions you might ask are: **¿Cuánto cuesta la entrada?** (how much do you charge for the admission?), **¿hay descuento para estudiantes?** (Is there a discount for students?), **¿puedo tomar fotos aquí?** (can I take pictures here?), **¿puedo contratar un guía?** (can I hire a guide?), **¿tiene folletos con información?** (do you have brochures with information?).

The names of places you would probably like to visit are: **museos** (museums), **monumentos** (landmarks), **parques** (parks), **parques de diversiones** (amusement parks), **calle**

principal (main square), **avenidas** (avenues), and more!

Some other vocabulary you might need is: **supermercado** (supermarket), **quiosco de periodicos** (newsstand), **casa de cambio** (exchange house), **librería** (bookstore), **panadería** (bakery), **farmacia** (drugstore), **policia** (police station), **parada de autobus** (bus stop), **parada de metro** (subway stop), **estacionamiento** (parking garage), **calle** (street), **letrero** (sign), among others.

Never forget when you ask anyone anything of any kind on the street or at some shop or place, to excuse you. If you forgot, we have seen in one of the previous chapters that you can say that with the words **disculpas** (I am sorry) and **perdoneme** (pardon me). And then you can go on with your question or your whatever you wish to. Finally, you should not forget to thank someone for giving you directions on any sort of help. If you remember, we have seen in the first chapter that you can say that by using the words **gracias** (thanks).

In this chapter, you have learned the necessary tools to get around a Spanish-speaking place. You can ask and understand directions, you can take a taxi, you know how to ask for touristic information in sights, and you know how are they called the things you would like to visit.

Keywords: **Tren** (train), **metro** (subway), **donde** (where), **calle** (street), **¿ a qué distancia esta?** (how far is it), **derecha** (right), **izquierda** (left), **derecho** (straight), **¿qué es eso?** (what is that?), **¿cuánto cuesta?** (how much is it), **museo** (museum).

Chapter 4: Eating

Now that you have done some sightseeing you must be getting hungry! Food and eating are not only essential for everyone, but it is also a significant part of getting to know a different culture. From food vocabulary to ways to ask things in restaurants, this chapter will help you succeed in any meal type situation using Spanish.

Getting to a restaurant

In case you are walking around and you want to know where to eat you should ask someone by saying, **¿Me puede recomendar un buen restaurante?** (Can you recommend me a good restaurant?) or **¿Hay un café cerca de aquí?** (Is there a cafe nearby?). You can also ask **¿Dónde se puede comer barato?** (where can you eat for a low price?) and **¿Cuál es la especialidad local?** (what is the local specialty?). Or you can even say **¿Donde esta el restaurante más cercano?** (where is the nearest restaurant?).

Communicating in eating situations

As you may imagine, two verbs are critical and strategical in order to express things about food, **comer** (eat) and **tomar** (drink). In previous chapters you have also learnt the verb **querer** (want) which will also be fundamental in this situations. You can express yourself to other Spanish speaking people by saying: **Tengo hambre** (I am hungry), **tengo sed** (I am thirsty) and **estoy lleno** (I am full). Moreover, **you can say tengo ganas de tomar un café** (I feel like drinking coffee), **tengo que comer algo** (I have to eat something) and **¿Tenes algo para tomar o para comer?** (do you have something to eat or drink). And if you want some more of something you just say **¡Más, por favor!** (more, please!) or if you want to say something is delicious you just say **¡Qué rico!** (delicious). Or if you are already full you can say **estoy lleno** (I am full).

Street food

In a lot of cities, there are different kind of street foods and meals which are delicious. If you happen to see a cart and do not understand what is exactly they sell you can ask them, **¿Qué tipo de comida se vende en este puesto?** (what sort of food is sold in this stand?). If you decided to eat something there, you could order by saying, **me da... ¿por favor?** (would you give me .... please?). In your case you should fill the order with what you want, for example, **me da una tortilla, ¿Por favor?** (would you give me a tortilla, please?). To drink you should ask **un vaso de... por favor** (a cup of ... please), for example, u**n vaso de cerveza por favor** (a cup of beer please).

If you have any doubts regarding the food you should say, **¿Qué es eso?** (what is that?). In some places, you might have to ask what they have that particular day or in general. You can do this really quickly by saying **¿Qué tiene de tomar?** (what do you have to drink?), **¿Que tiene hoy para comer?** (what do you have to eat today?) or **¿Qué sabores tiene de...?** (What flavors do you have of...?), for example, **¿qué sabores tiene de helado?** (what ice cream flavors do you have?). You might also want to ask for cutlery by saying **¿Me podría dar un tenedor?** (can you give me a fork?) or you can ask **¿Me podría dar una servilleta?** (can you give me a napkin).

At a restaurant

When you get to a restaurant, you might want to know if there are any tables available, to address this you say, **¿Tenes una mesa?** (Do you have a table?). You can also ask for the number of people you want to eat with, for example, **¿Tenes una mesa para cuatro?** (do you have a table for four?). In case you need to wait you may ask, **¿ Cuánto hay de espera?** (how long do we have to wait?). Another thing you can do is book in advance and to do this, you need to say **quisiera reservar una mesa para... a las ...** (I would like to book a table for... at...). For example, you say **quisiera reservar una mesa para dos a las nueve** (I would like to book a table for two at nine o'clock).

Other preferences in a table at a restaurant may include: **quisieramos sentarnos junto a la ventana** (we would like to seat by the window), **¿ tenes una mesa en el área no fumador?** (do you have a table in the non-smoking area?), **¿puedo fumar acá?** (can I smoke in here?) and **¿me traerías un cenicero por favor?** (can you bring me an ashtray, please?).

Ordering your food in Spanish is not difficult at all. However, if you cannot understand the menu you can ask **¿tiene un menú en inglés?** (do you have a menu in English?), and further requests like, **¿tiene un menú infantil?** (do you have a children's menu?) or **¿tiene algún plato vegetariano?** (do you have a vegetarian dish?). Furthermore, you can ask the waiter **¿qué recomienda?** (what do you recommend?), **¿Qué tiene ese plato?** (what is in that dish?) or **¿Con qué se acompaña ese plato?** (what does that plate come with?). When you decided what you want to eat you just ask for **una orden de...** (an order of) and your desired meal. For example, **una orden de fideos, por favor** (an order of spaghetti, please).

When you finish your meal, you can ask for the bill by saying, **eso es todo** (that is all) and **la cuenta, por favor** (the check, please). You can also ask if they accept credit cards by saying **¿aceptan tarjetas de credito?** (do you accept credit cards?) and you can ask if the tip is included by saying, **¿la cuenta incluye propina?** (Is the tip included in the bill?).

Ordering drinks

While you are eating, or at any time, you are going to want to drink something, and you should know how to do it. For any type of drink, you ask for **un vaso de/una taza de** (a glass of/a cup of), for example **un vaso de agua** (a glass of water) or **una taza de cafe** (a cup of coffee). You can ask for things **con hielo** (with ice) or **sin hielo** (with no ice). If you want to call for a whole bottle you order a **botella** (a bottle), for example, **una botella de vino tinto, por favor** (a bottle of red wine, please).

Basic food vocabulary

Here is some basic vocabulary you might need to know either to order food or to buy food. First, the kinds of foods are **primer plato** (appetizers), **plato principal** (main dish) and **postre** (dessert). You also have **desayuno** (breakfast), **almuerzo** (lunch) and **cena** (dinner).

You might also need to know the names of several beverages like **cerveza** (beer), **cafe** (coffee), **jugo** (juice), **jugo de naranja** (orange juice), **agua mineral** (mineral water), **te** (tea). And a number of foods like **sopa** (soup), **ensalada** (salad), **pan** (bread), **manteca** (butter), **fideos** (noodles), **arroz** (rice), **queso** (cheese), **verduras** (vegetables), **pollo** (chicken), **cerdo** (pork), **carne** (meat).

If you want to order meat, you should also know how to ask for it. If you want your steak to be rare you ask for **la carne poco cocida** and if you want it medium you ask for **la carne a medio cocer**. Finally, if you want it well-done you ask for **la carne bien cocida**.

The types of foods are **picante** (spicy), **dulce** (sweet) or **amargo** (sour). And the utensils on the dining table are **platos** (plates), **tenedor** (fork), **cuchillo** (knife), **cuchara** (spoon),

servilleta (napkin), **taza** (cup), **vaso** (glass), **sal** (salt), **pimienta** (pepper) and **azucar** (sugar).

In this chapter you have learned how to get around different kinds of eating situations. From eating in the street to having a meal in a fancy restaurant, you can handle anything with your Spanish skills. Among other things, you can ask for restaurant recommendations, how to communicate in dining situations, how to order foods in the street and how to ask for tables at restaurants. Furthermore, you know how to order at a restaurant, how to order drinks and several words that build your culinary vocabulary such as names of food and to say how you prefer your meat.

Keywords: **comida** (food), **hambriento** (hungry), **restaurante** (restaurant), **mesa** (table), **me da...** (would you give me), **un vaso** de... (a glass of), **¿tiene un menu en ingles?** (do you have a menu in English?), **la cuenta** (the check), **cafe** (coffee), **agua** (water), **cerveza** (beer), **carne** (meat), **pollo** (chicken), **fideos** (noodles), **ensalada** (salad).

Chapter 5: Shopping

Whether you are staying just a few days, a couple of weeks or some months in you Spanish speaking destination, eventually you will need to buy some things. This chapter will help you to succeed in any time of buying situation from buying food and clothes to buying remedies and medicines.

Communicating in shopping situations

At any kind of interaction that implies some buying, there are some phrases which are crucial. An extremely necessary phrase is **¿cuánto cuesta?** (how much does it cost?). By itself that phrase is clear and efficient but if you want to be more specific you can say, for example, **¿cuánto cuesta la remera?** (how much is the t shirt?). Another important information you might need to ask is **¿a qué hora abre la tienda?** (what time does the store open?) or **¿a qué hora cierra la tienda?** (what time does the store close?). Or, **¿puedo pagar con tarjeta de crédito?** (can I pay with credit card?), **¿puedo pagar con efectivo?** (can I pay with cash?) and **¿puedo ordenar esto por internet?** (can I order this online?).

Furthermore, you can be asked some questions by the sellers like **¿necesita alguna ayuda?** (can I help you?) or **¿ qué esta buscando?** (what are you looking for?). To that you can reply, **necesito/quiero esto…** (I need/want this…) or **estoy buscando…** (I am looking for…) and complete with your information, for example, **necesito un buzo** (I need a sweatshirt), **quiero un pantalon** (I want some pants) or **estoy buscando un remedio para la tos** (I am looking for a cough remedy). After that the seller will bring your desired item and say, **acá esta** (here it is) and **¿eso es todo?** (is that all?).

Shopping for food

When you need to buy some food, the most common place to go is the supermarket. If you are looking for one you can ask **¿dónde está el supermercado más cercano?** (where is the nearest supermarket?) or **¿cómo llego al supermercado?** (how do I get to the supermarket?).

Once you are there, you may need to know where things are. These are simple phrases that will help you get around any kind of food shopping place. For example, **¿en qué pasillo está el arroz?** (in which aisle is the rice?) and you can change the ending of you question easily to ask for any other product like **¿ en qué**

pasillo está la mantequilla? (in which aisle is the butter?). Also you may ask **¿dónde está la sección de lácteos?** (where is the dairy section?) or **¿dónde está la sección de carnes?** (where is the meat section?).

At your desired supermarket section, you should know how to ask and order things. For example, if you are looking for some bread you might ask **¿está fresco el pan?** (is the bread fresh?) and **¿me daría unas rodajas de pan?** (would you give me some slices of bread?). Then, you can ask how much things are by their weight, for example, **¿cuanto cuesta un kilo de tomate?** (how much is a kilo of tomatoes?) or **¿cuánto cuesta un kilo de pan?** (how much is it a kilo of bread?). As you can see, making this question is really easy and you can change the last word according to your asking needs. Other questions that may rise to you might be if there are other kinds of things, for example, **¿tiene otros tipos de te?** (do you have other kinds of tea?) or **¿tiene otros tipos de queso?** (do you have other kinds of cheese?).

In case you have to order the food in specific parts of the supermarket you can say **quisiera 3 rebanadas de queso** (I would like three slices of cheese) or **quiero un kilo de carne** (I want a kilo of meat). If you want some more you can say **un poco más, por favor** (more, please) or, if you don't, you say **ya esta bien, gracias** (it is enough, thanks).

Further on, some questions regarding the prices might come up like **¿dónde está el lector de precios?** (where is the price scanner?) or **no tengo cambio** (I do not have change). Also when you pay for your things you may need to ask **¿me podría dar una bolsa por favor?** (can you give me a bag please?).

Shopping for clothes

When you go into a clothes store there are some certain phrases you should know. For example, if someone asks you **¿necesita ayuda?** (do you need help?) you can either answer **solo estoy mirando** (i am just looking) o **si, porfavor** (yes, please). Then if you see any clothes you like you can ask to try them on by saying **¿me lo puedo probar?** (can I try it on?) or you can ask for an specific size by saying **¿tiene talla mediana?** (do you have a medium size?) or **¿tiene talla grande?** (do you have a large size?). And if you want to ask for shoe sizes you can say **¿tiene estos zapatos en número ocho?** (do you have this shoes in size eight?), and change the number according to your shoe size.

As you are trying clothes you can either say **es demasiado chico** (It is too small), **es demasiado grande** (It is too big), **no me queda bien** (It does not fit) or **me queda perfecto** (It fits perfectly). Moreover, regarding the prices you can say **es muy caro** (it is too expensive) or **¿tiene algo más barato?** (do you have something cheaper?). And if you want to return something you bought you can say **quisiera devolver eso** (I would like to return this).

Some clothing vocabulary that might be useful to you is: **ropa para mujeres** (women's clothes), **ropa para hombres** (men´s clothes), **blusa** (blouse), **falda** (pollera), **vestido** (dress), **pantalones** (pants), **camisa** (shirt), **zapatos** (shoes) and **medias** (socks).

Shopping for medicines

In case anything happens, you should always know how to ask for things at the pharmacy, at the hospital or at the clinic. For example, if you go to the pharmacy you can say **necesito algo para...** (I need something for...) and you insert your pain here, for example, **necesito algo para el dolor de cabeza** (I need something for a headache) or **necesito algo para el dolor de garganta** (I need something for a throatache). You can tell the pharmacist or the doctor if something is **leve** (light) or **grave** (serious). Also you can ask them referring to the medicine, **¿cuantas veces al día lo tomo?** (how many times a day do I take it?).

Moreover, if you are looking for some stuff at the pharmacy you may ask **¿ en que sección estan...?** (in which section are the...) or **busco...** (I am looking for...) and you can add

whatever it is you are looking for, for example,
¿en qué sección está el protector solar? (in which section is the sunscreen?) or **estoy buscando palillos de algodón** (I am looking for q-tips). You can also ask whether they are selling something you want by saying **¿hay…?** (do you sell…?), for example, **¿hay alcohol antiséptico?** (do you sell rubbing alcohol?).

In this chapter you have learned to get around shopping situations in the Spanish language. Now you can go and shop for food, clothes, medicines and much more! These were some essential and daily shopping situations but you can use the same vocabulary to buy almost everything. You know how to ask for things at the supermarket, how to know where to find things at the supermarket, know how to ask for clothes and how to respond to sellers, how to speak about clothes, how to ask for different types of medicines and toiletries and buy things at the pharmacy, among many others.

Key words: **¿cuanto cuesta?** (how much is it?), **estoy buscando…** (I am looking for), **remera** (t shirt), **pantalón** (pant), **vestido** (dress), **rebanadas** (slices), **¿ en que pasillo está…?** (in which aisle is…?), **zapatos** (shoes), **solo estoy mirando** (I am just looking around), **necesito algo para el dolor de cabeza** (I need something for a headache), **¿ cuántas veces al día lo tomo?** (how many times a day do I take it?), **¿hay (...)?** (do you sell...?).

Glossary: Common Useful Words

Agua: water.

Asiento: seat.

Ayuda: help.

Cafe: coffee.

Calle: street.

Carne: meat.

Cerveza: beer.

Comida: food.

Derecha: right.

Derecho: straight.

Disculpas: I am sorry.

Dónde: where.

Ensalada: salad.

Equipaje de mano: carry-on luggage.

Estoy buscando (…): I am looking for (...).
For example, **estoy buscando un restaurante**
(I am looking for a restaurant).

Estoy perdido: I am lost.

Fideos: noodles/spaghettis.

Gracias: thank you.

Habitación: room.

Hambriento: hungry.

Hola: hello.

Izquierda: left.

La cuenta: the check

Maleta: suitcase/luggage.

Me da (…): can you give me (...). For example, **me da un kilo de pan, porfavor** (can you give me a kilo of bread please).

Mesa: table.

Metro: subway.

Museo: museum.

Necesito algo para el dolor de cabeza: I need something for a headache.

No: no.

Noches: nights.

Pantalón: pant.

Pollo: chicken.

Por favor: please.

Rebanadas: slices.

Remera: t shirt.

Restaurante: restaurant.

Si: yes.

Solo estoy mirando: I am just looking around.

Terminal: terminal

Tren: train

Un vaso de (…): a glass of (...). For example,
un vaso de agua (a glass of water).

Vestido: dress

Zapatos: shoes

¿A qué distancia esta?: how far is it?

¿Cuántas veces al día lo tomo?: how many
times a day do I take it?

¿En qué pasillo está (…)?: in which aisle is (…)? For example, **¿en qué pasillo está la carne?** (in which aisle is the meat?).

¿Cuánto cuesta?: how much is it?

¿Cómo estás?: how are you?

¿Hay (…)?: Do you sell (…)? For example, **¿hay queso azul?** (do you sell blue cheese?).

¿Me podrías ayudar?: can you help me?

¿Podría llamarme un taxi?: can you call me a taxi?

¿Qué es eso?: what is that?

¿Tiene un menu en ingles?: do you have a menu in English?

Conclusion

Dear reader, thank you for exploring this book and sticking around until the very end. I hope this book has lived up to your expectations!

Whether you are going for work or pleasure to your Spanish speaking destination, you know how to handle almost every situation. From the airport and the hotel, to getting around and sightseeing, and finally eating and buying all sorts of things, you can do all of it in Spanish.

With just a little practice and putting this book into use, you will become a Spanish pro in no time!

I whish you the best of luck!